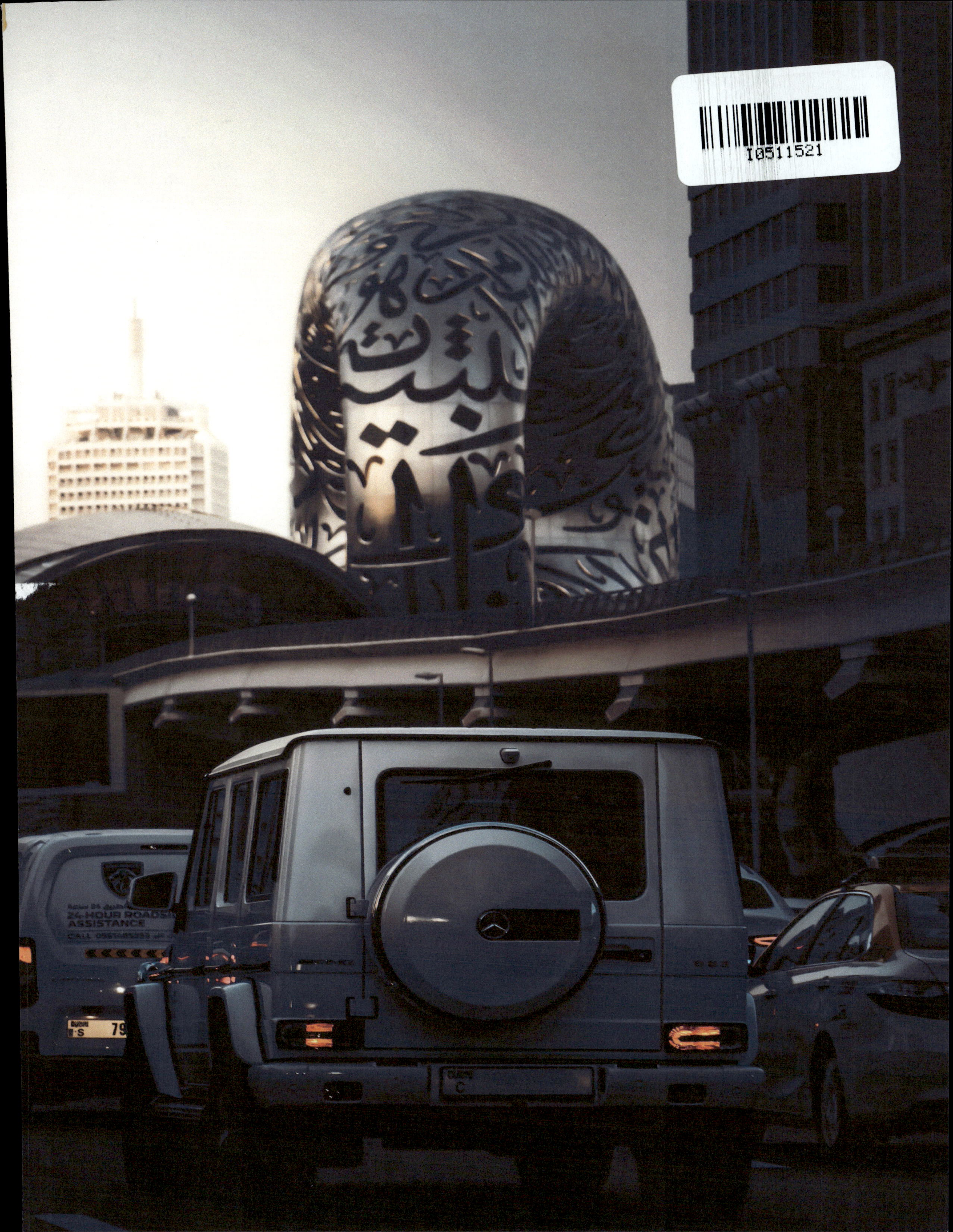
24-HOUR ROADS
ASSISTANCE

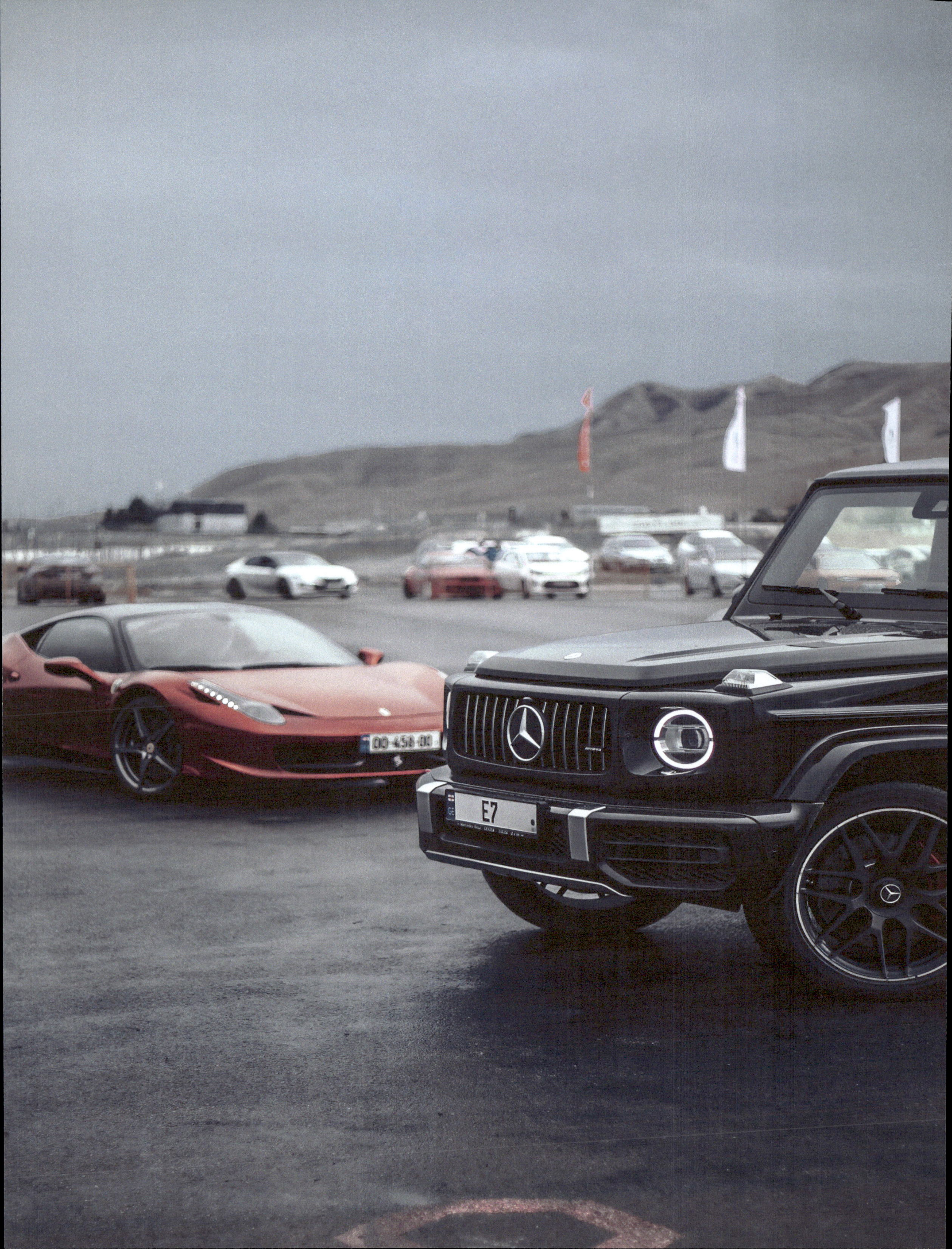
E7

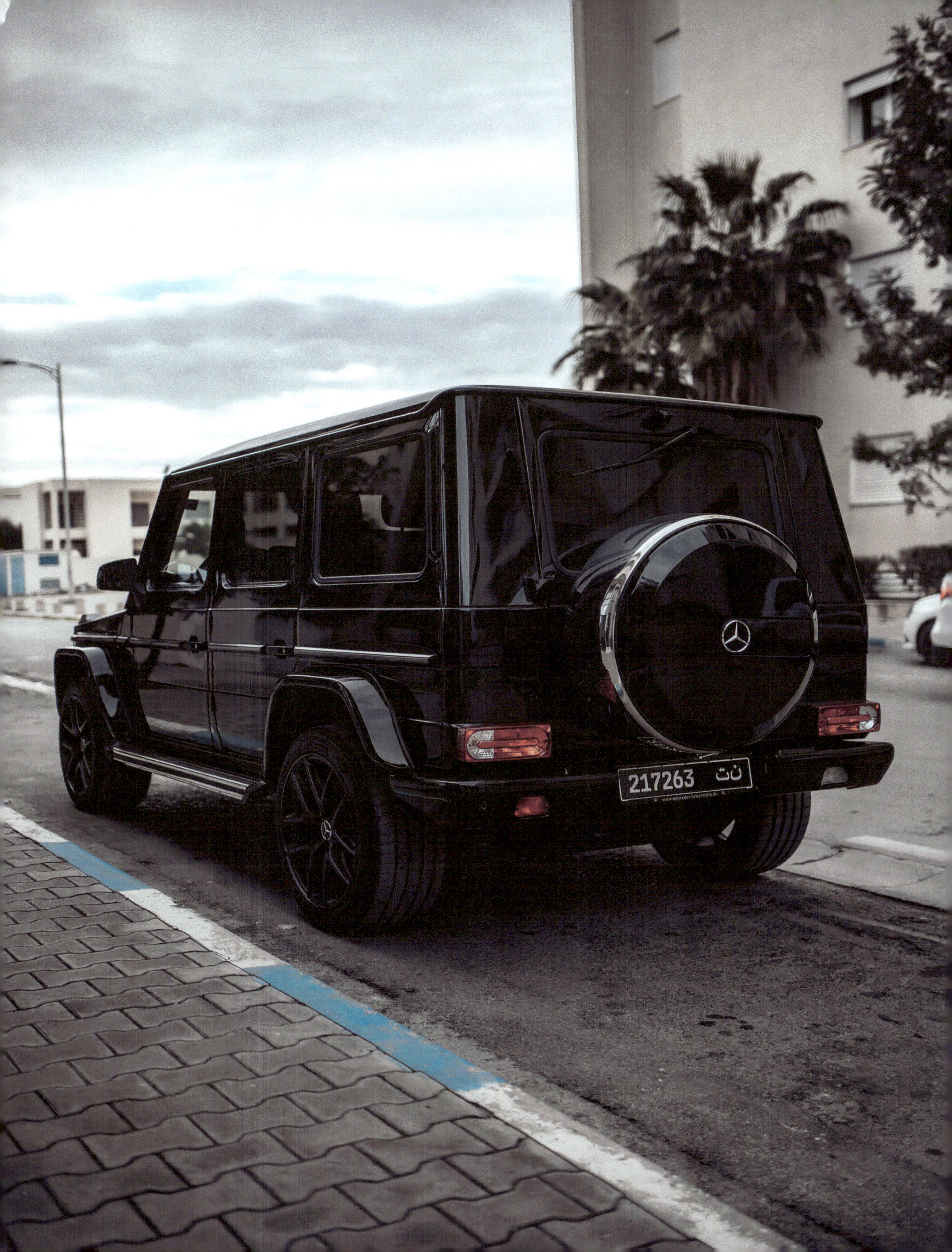
217263

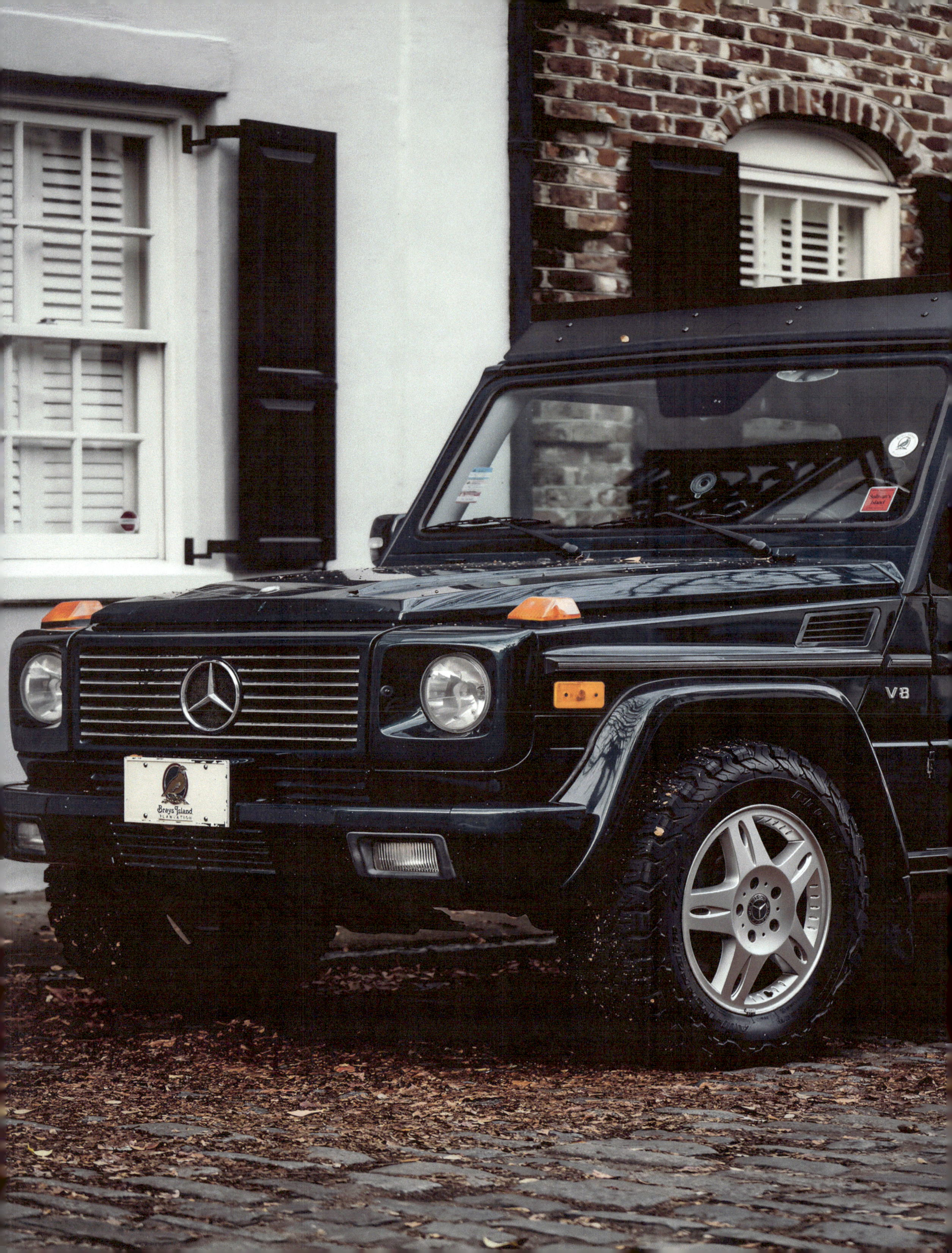
V8
Brays Island
PLANTATION

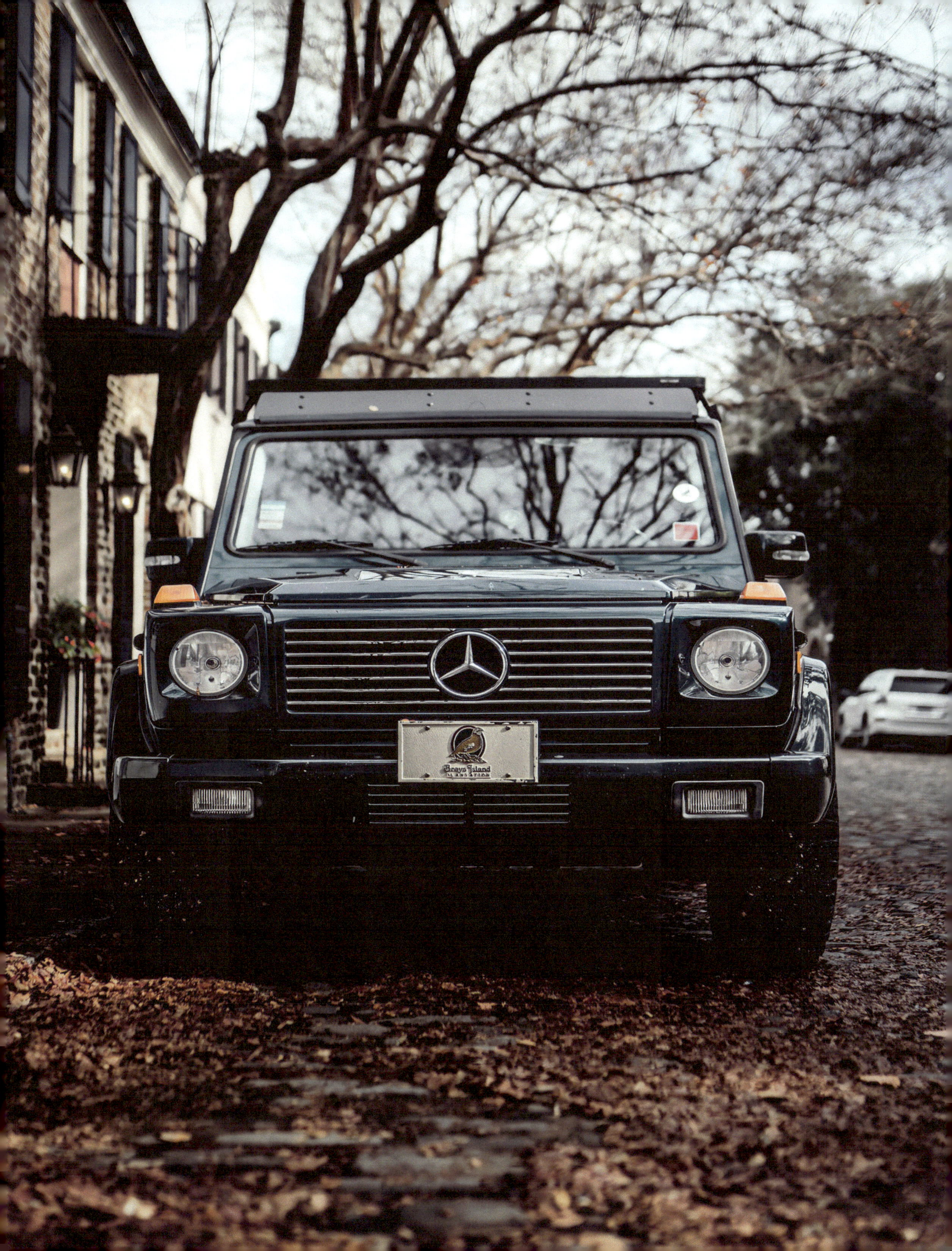
Brays Island

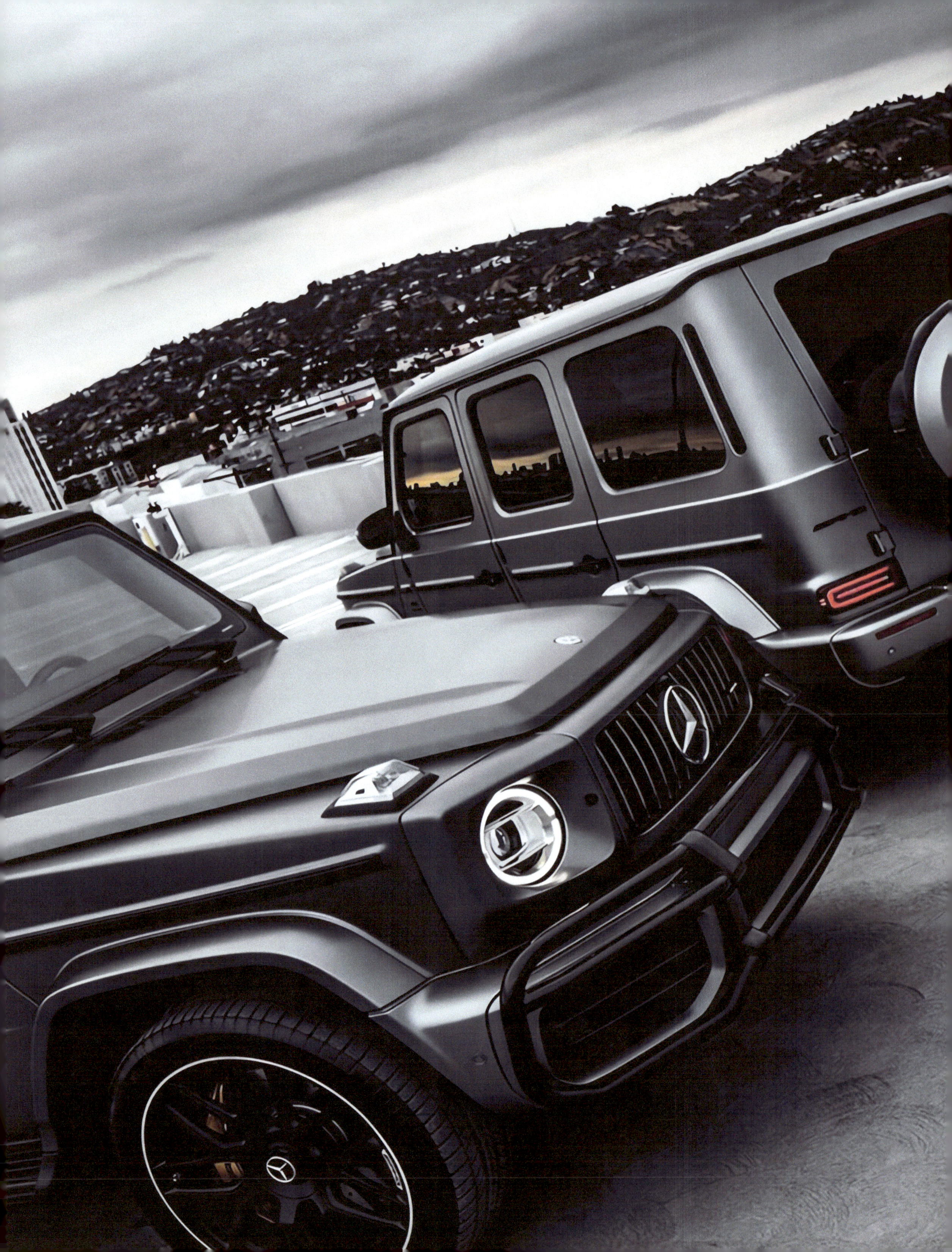

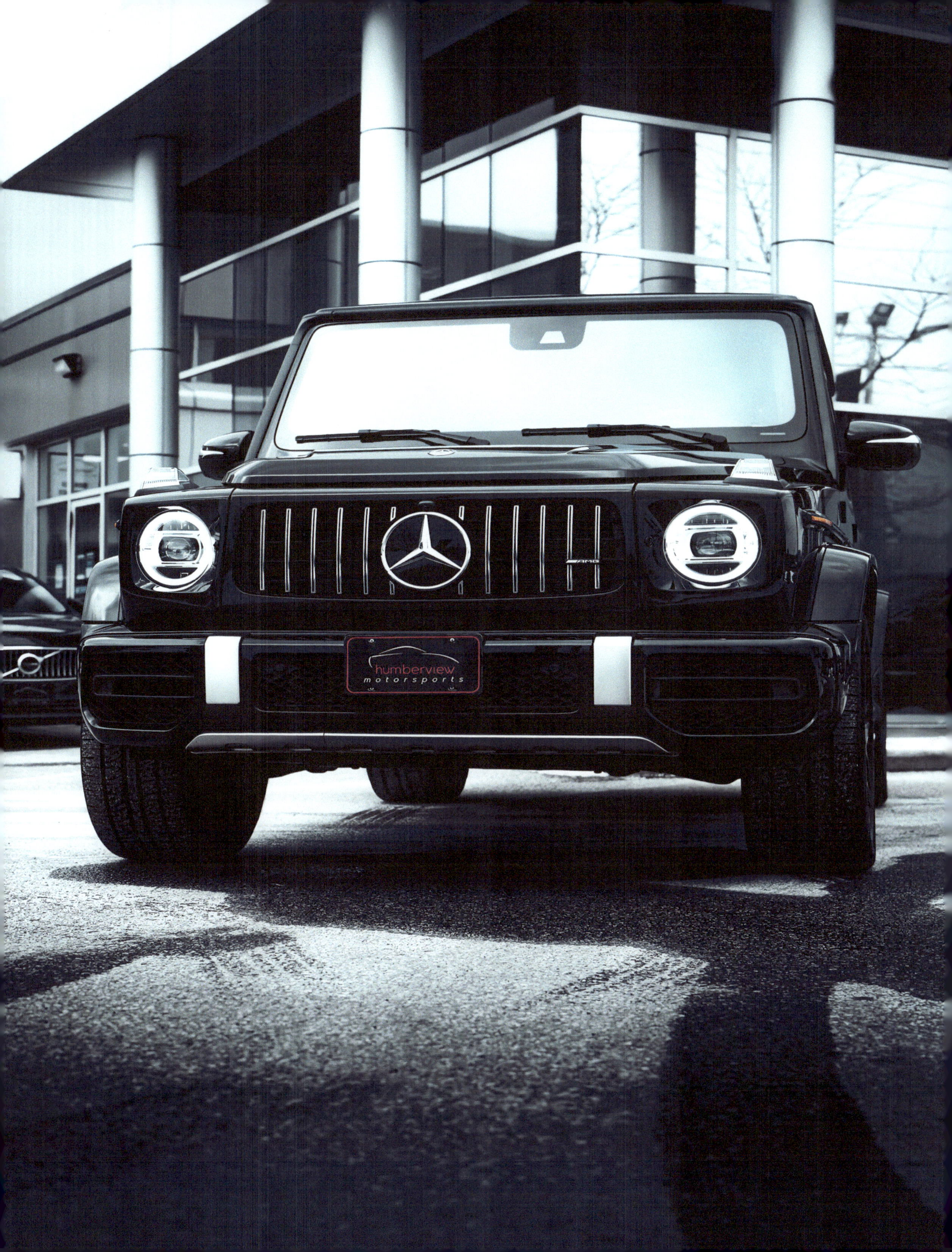
humberview
motorsports

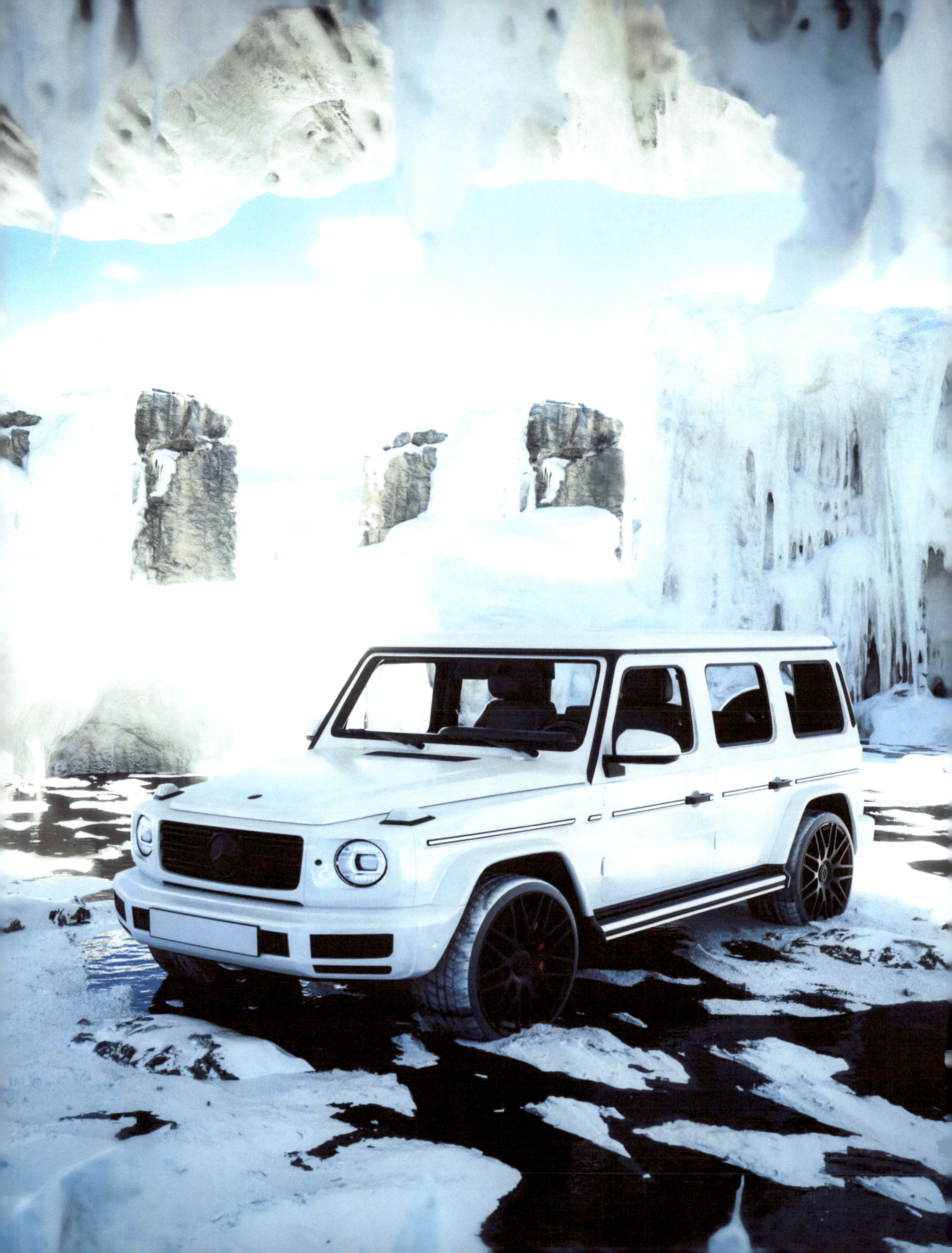

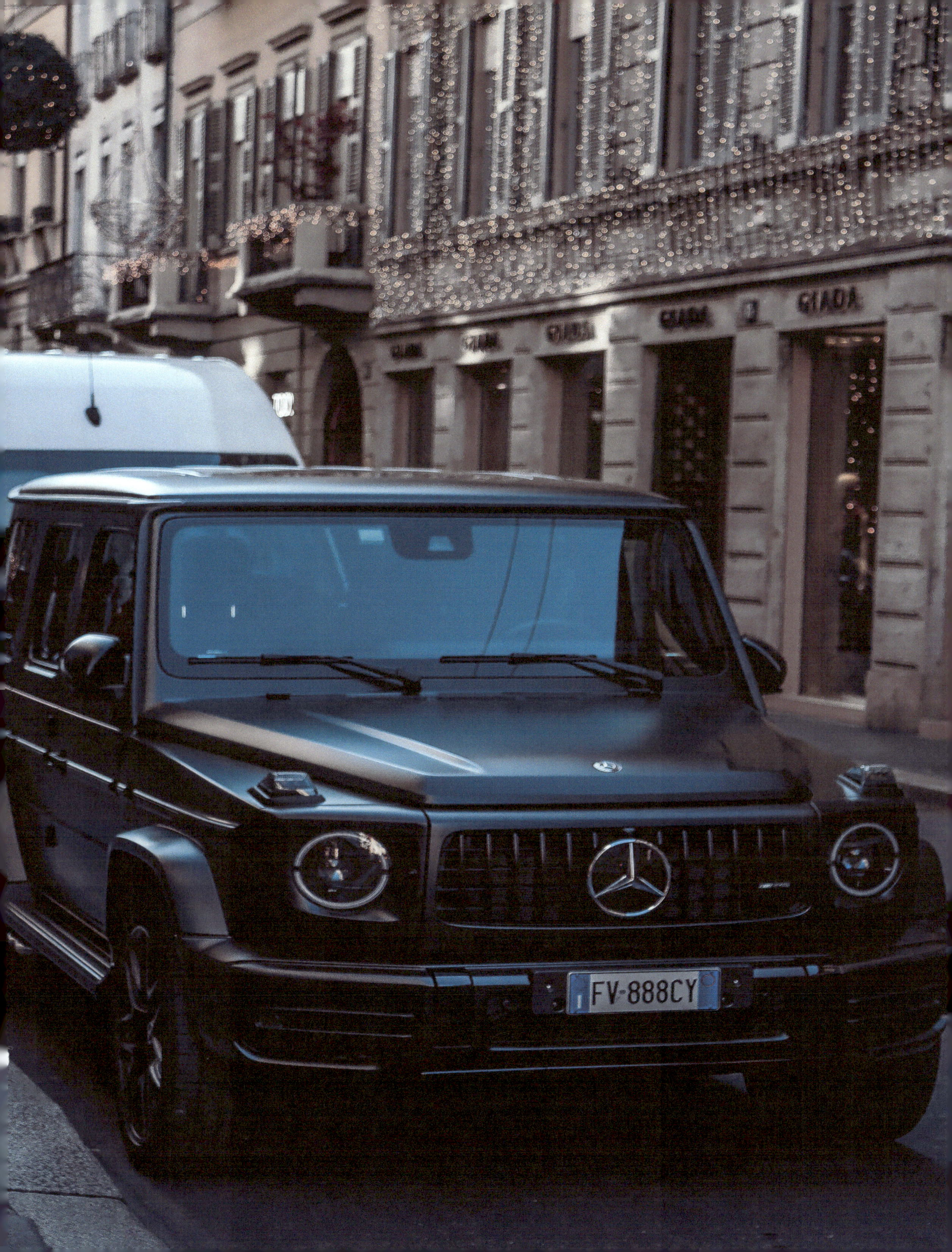
GIADA
FV-888CY

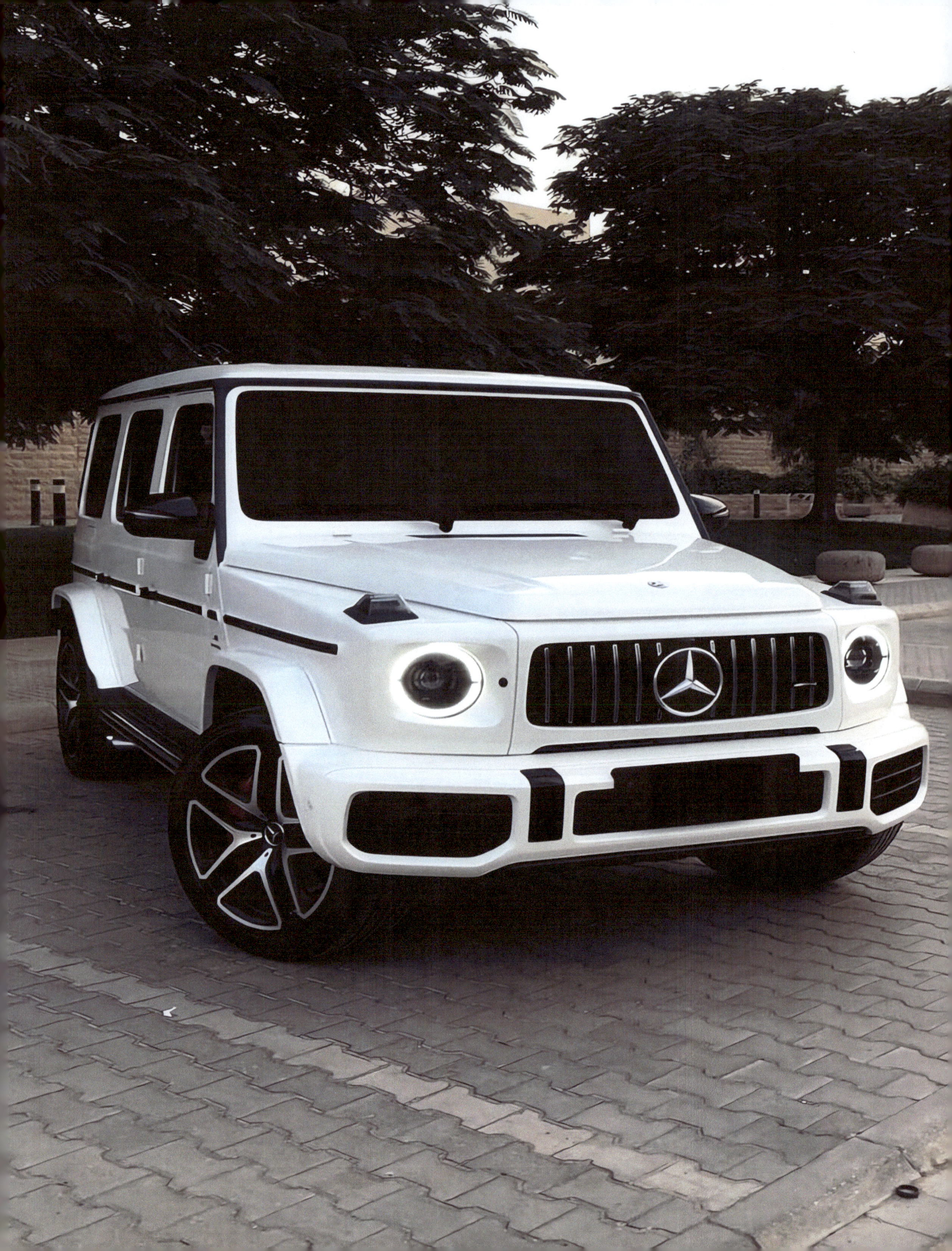

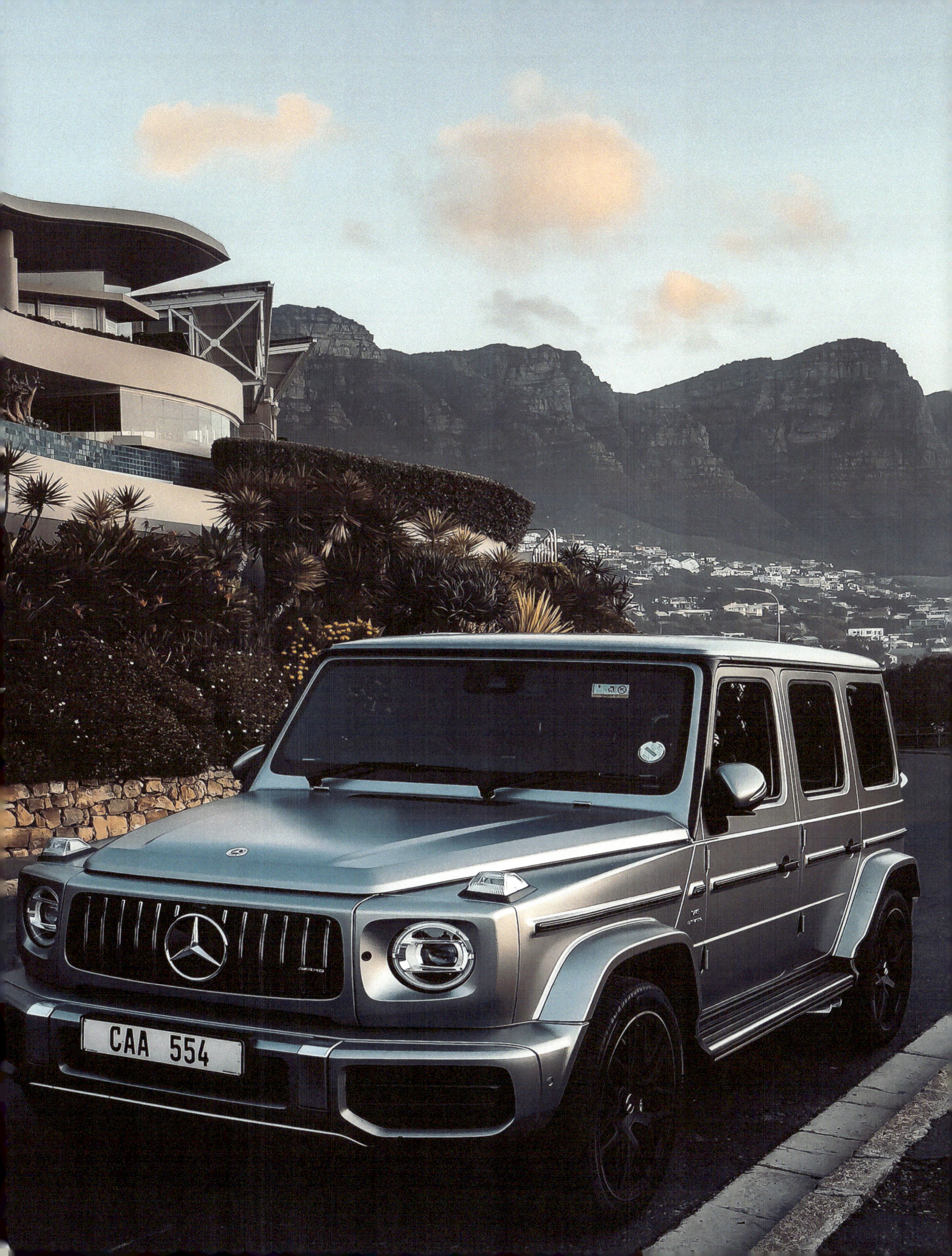
CAA 554

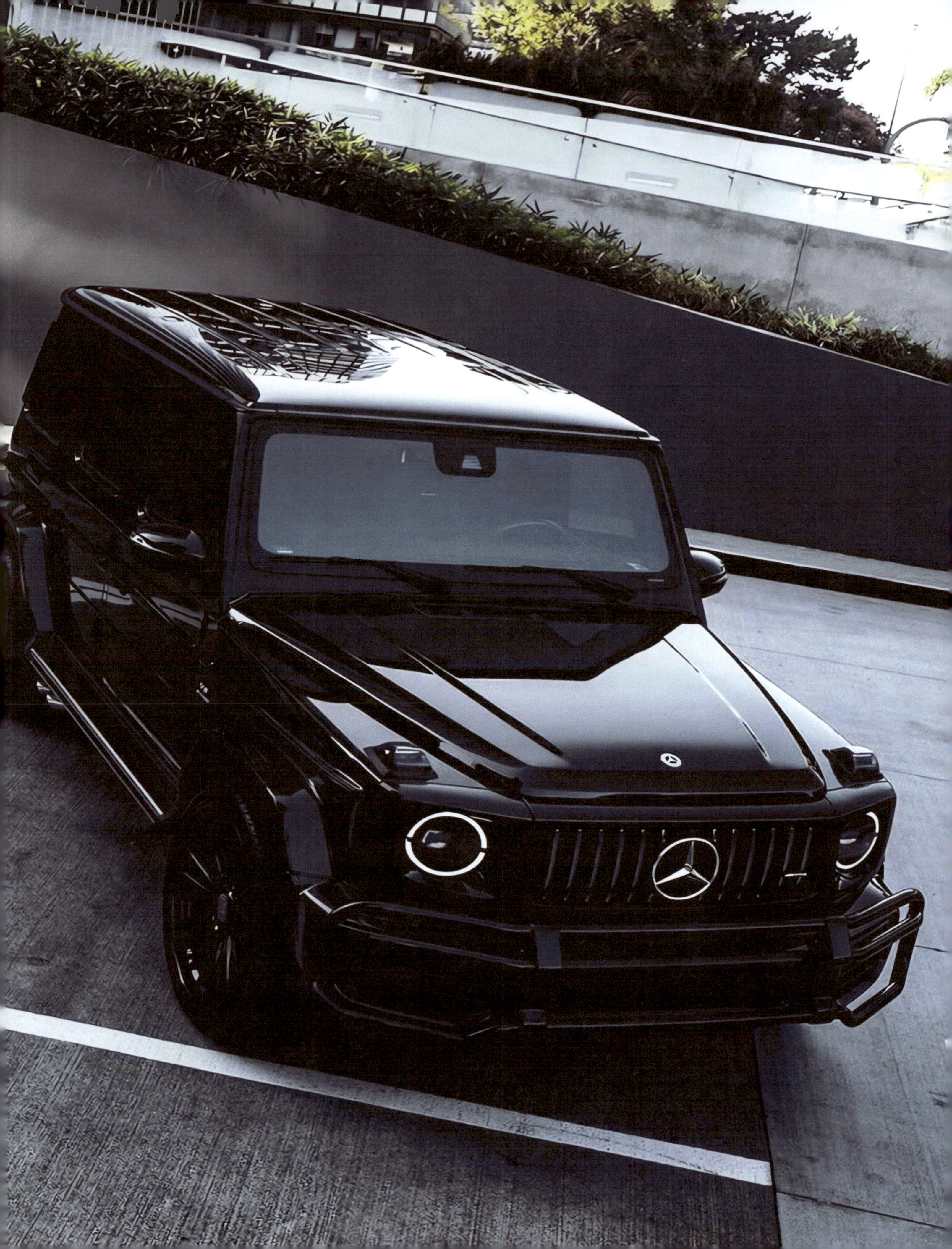

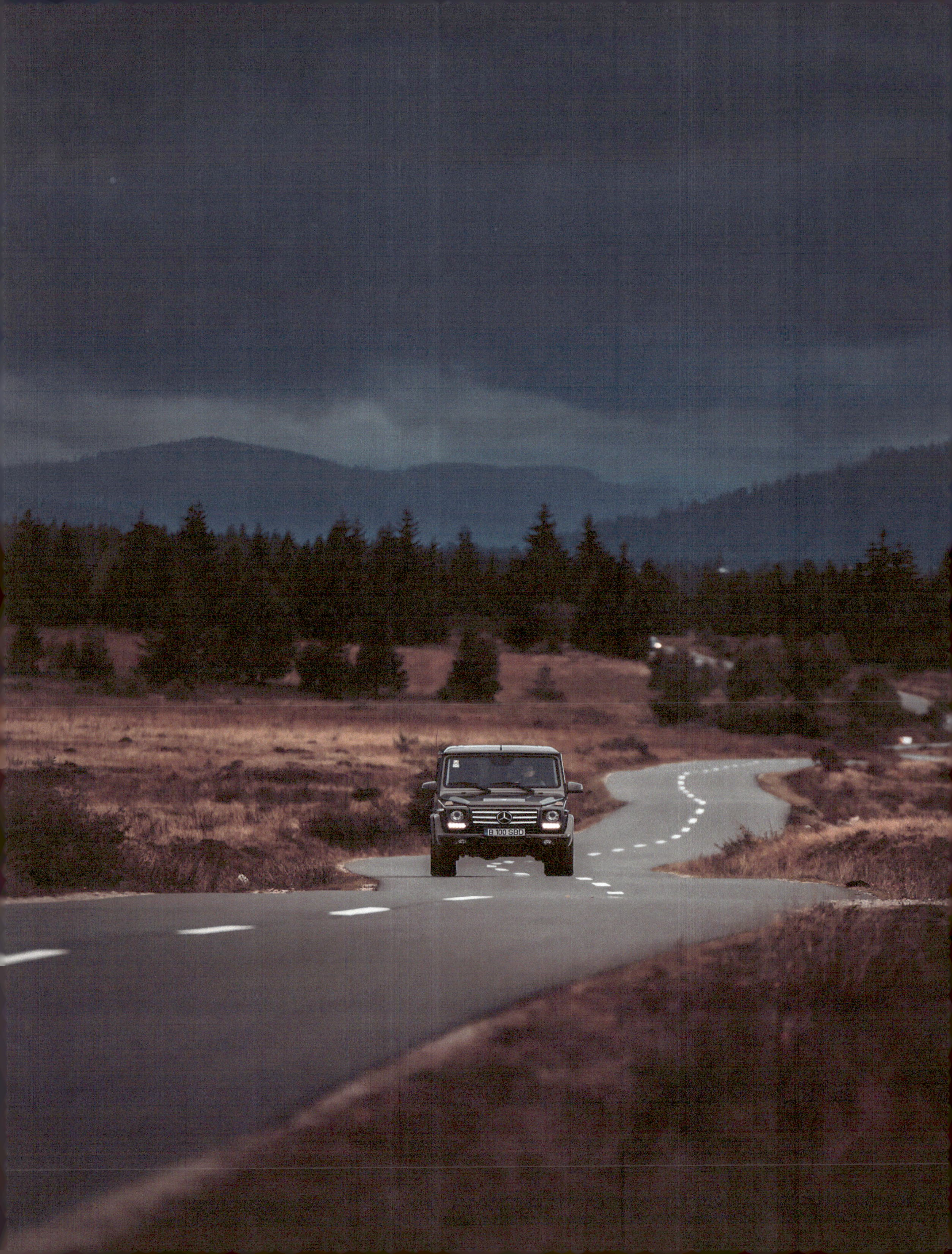
B 100 SBD

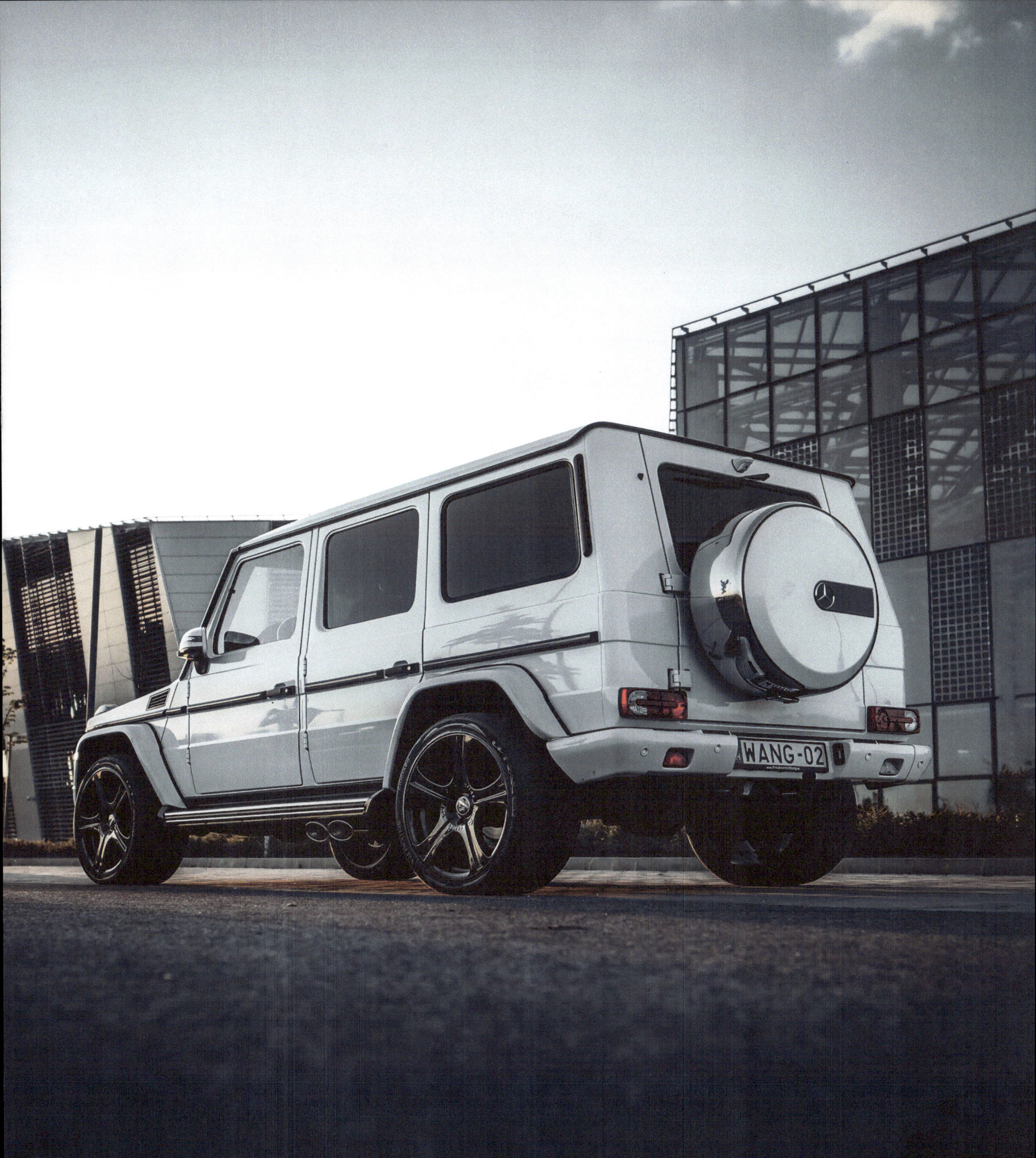
WANG-02

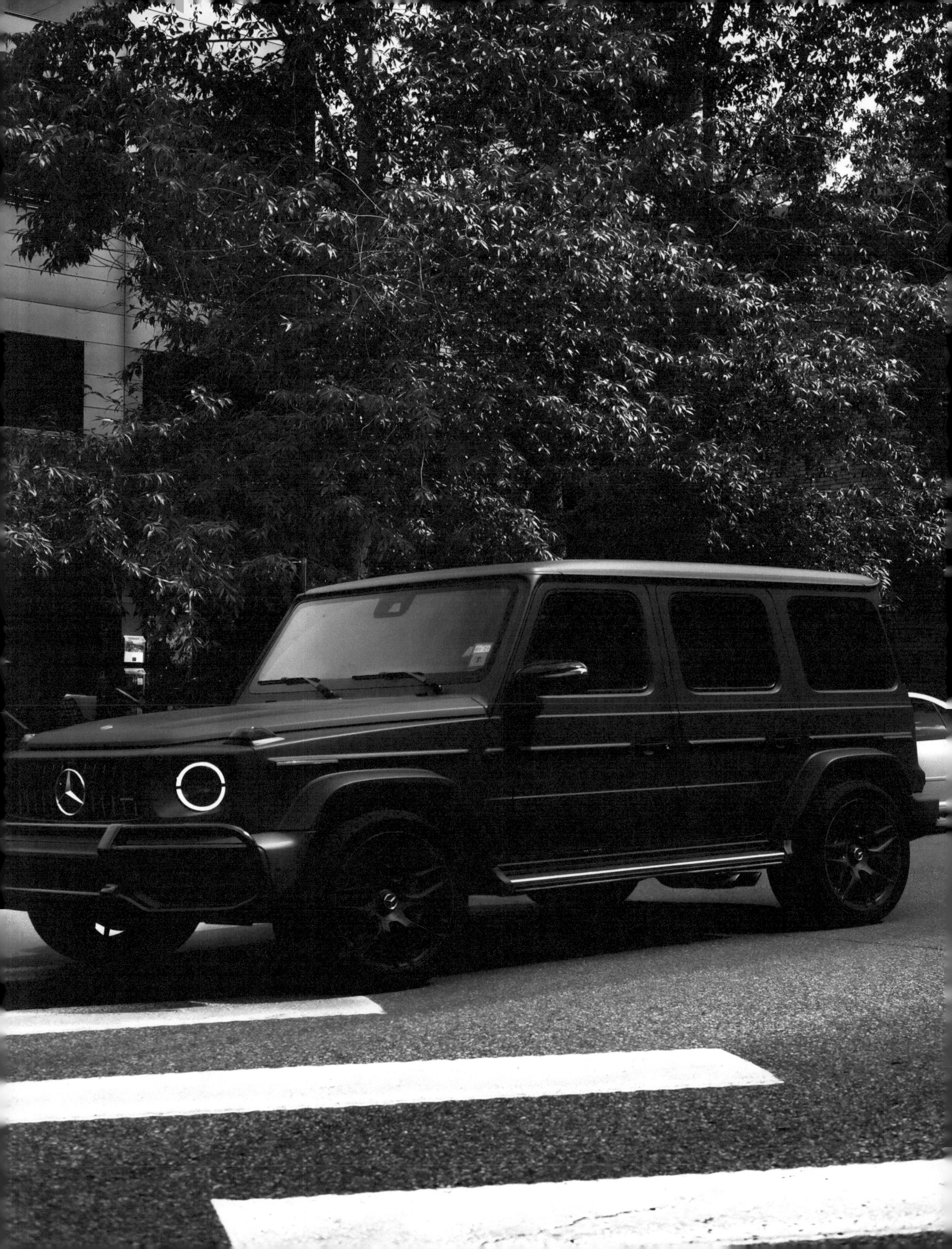

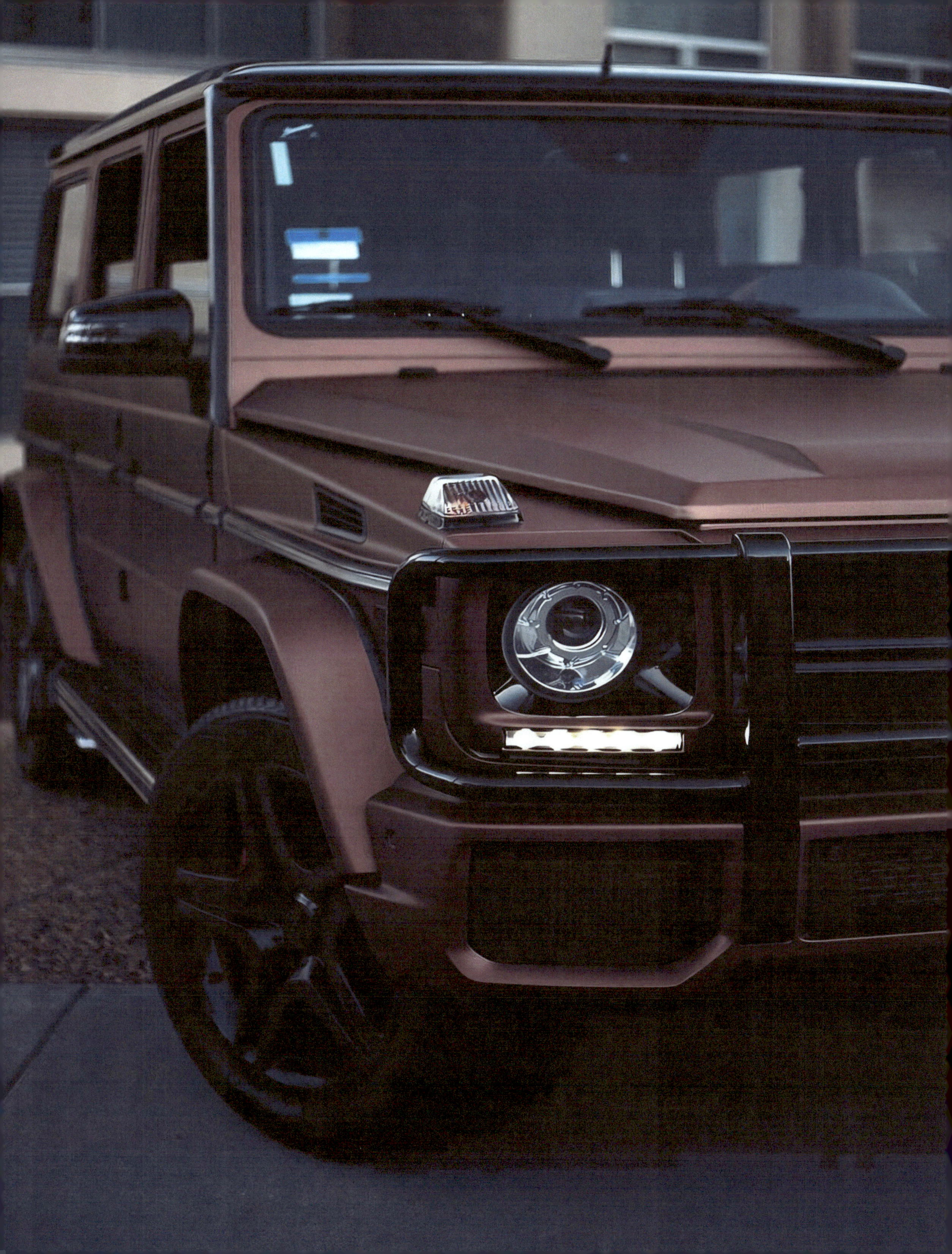

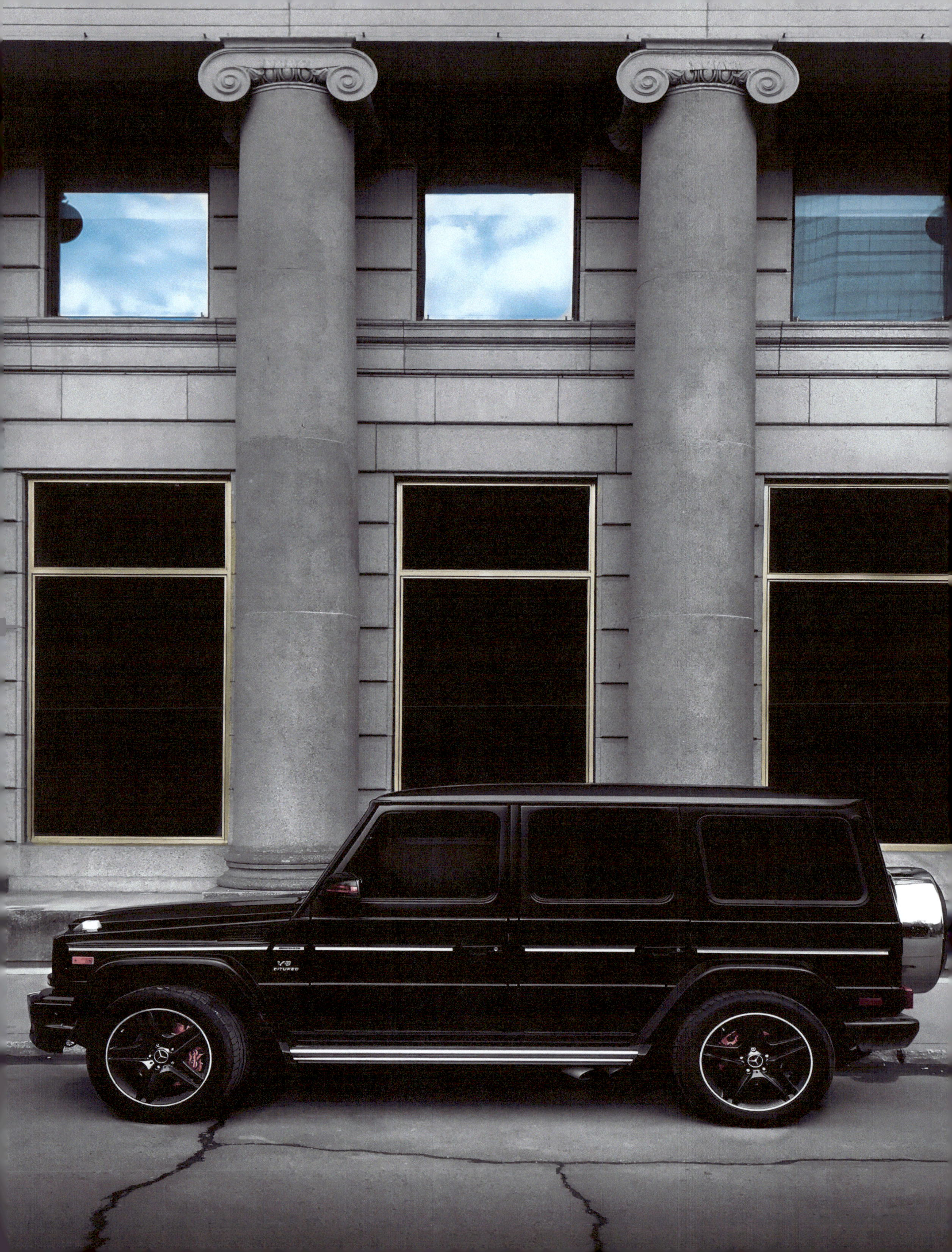

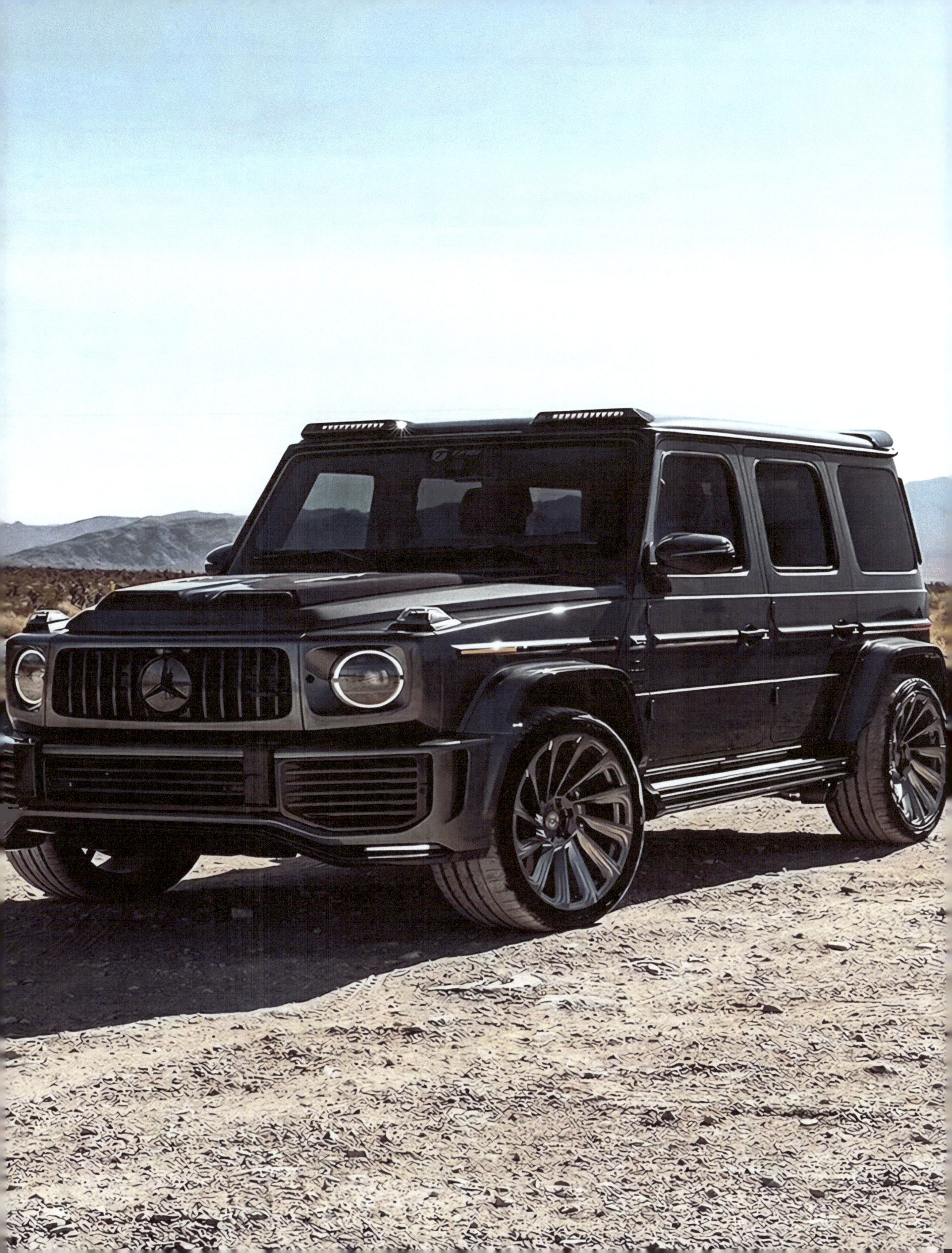

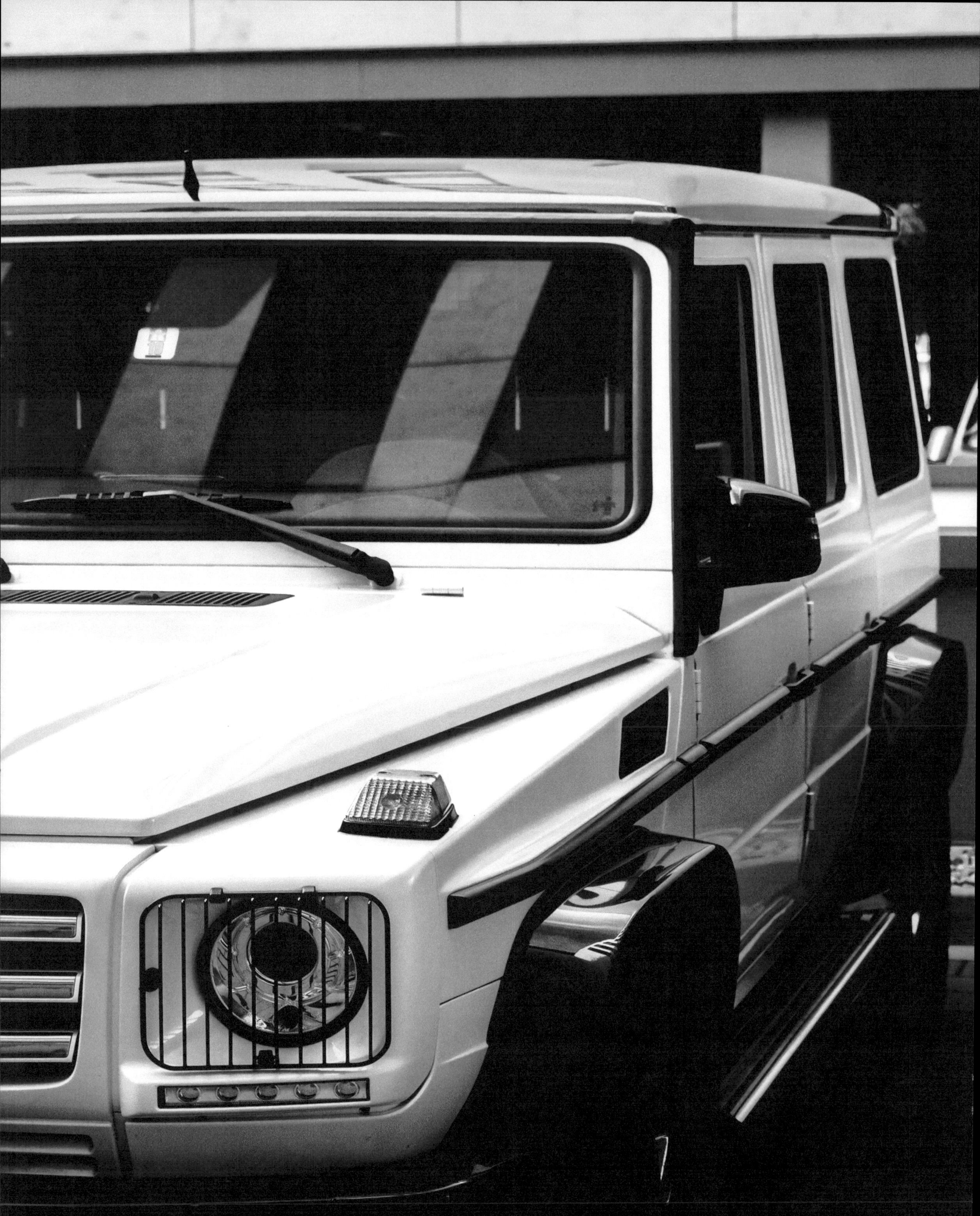

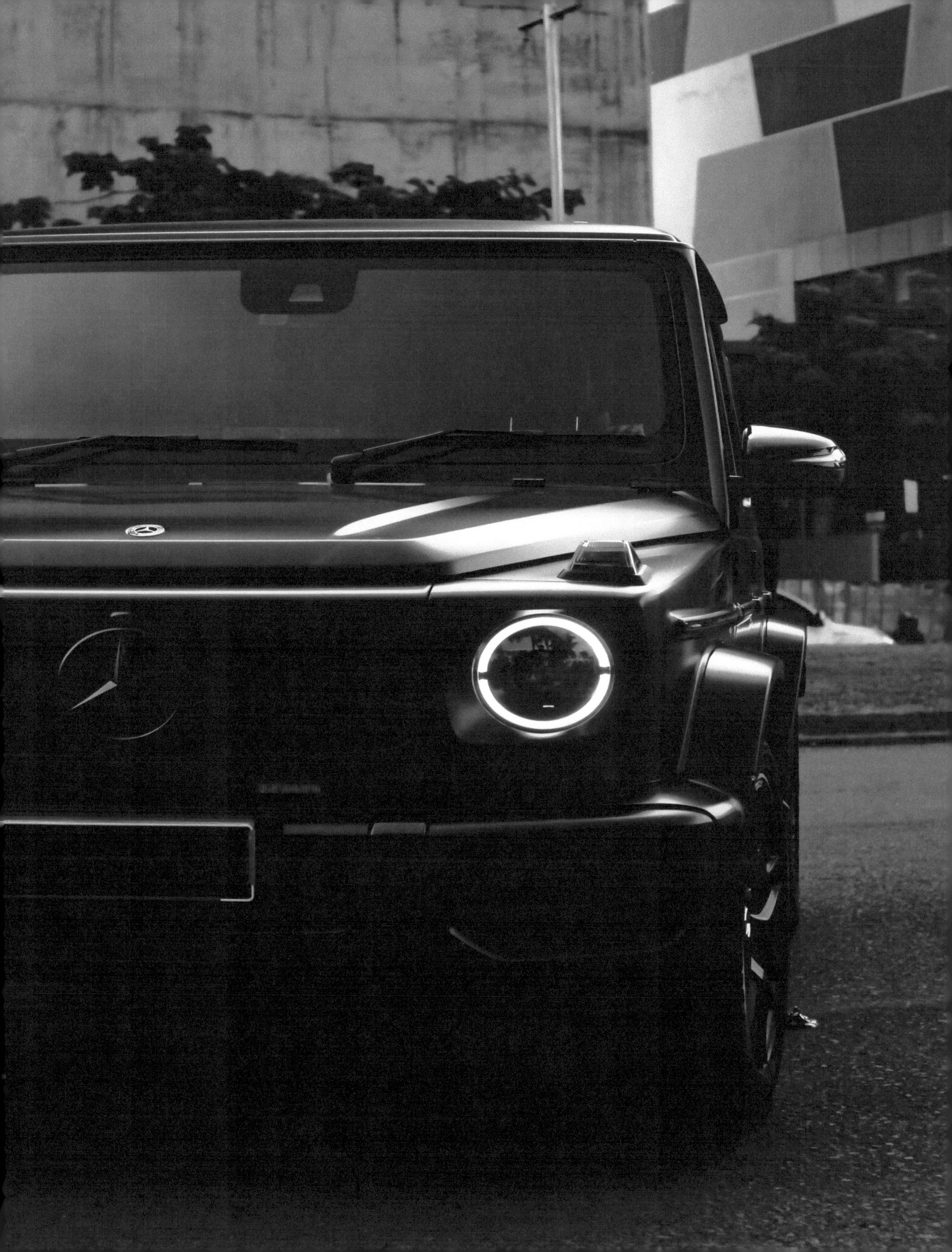

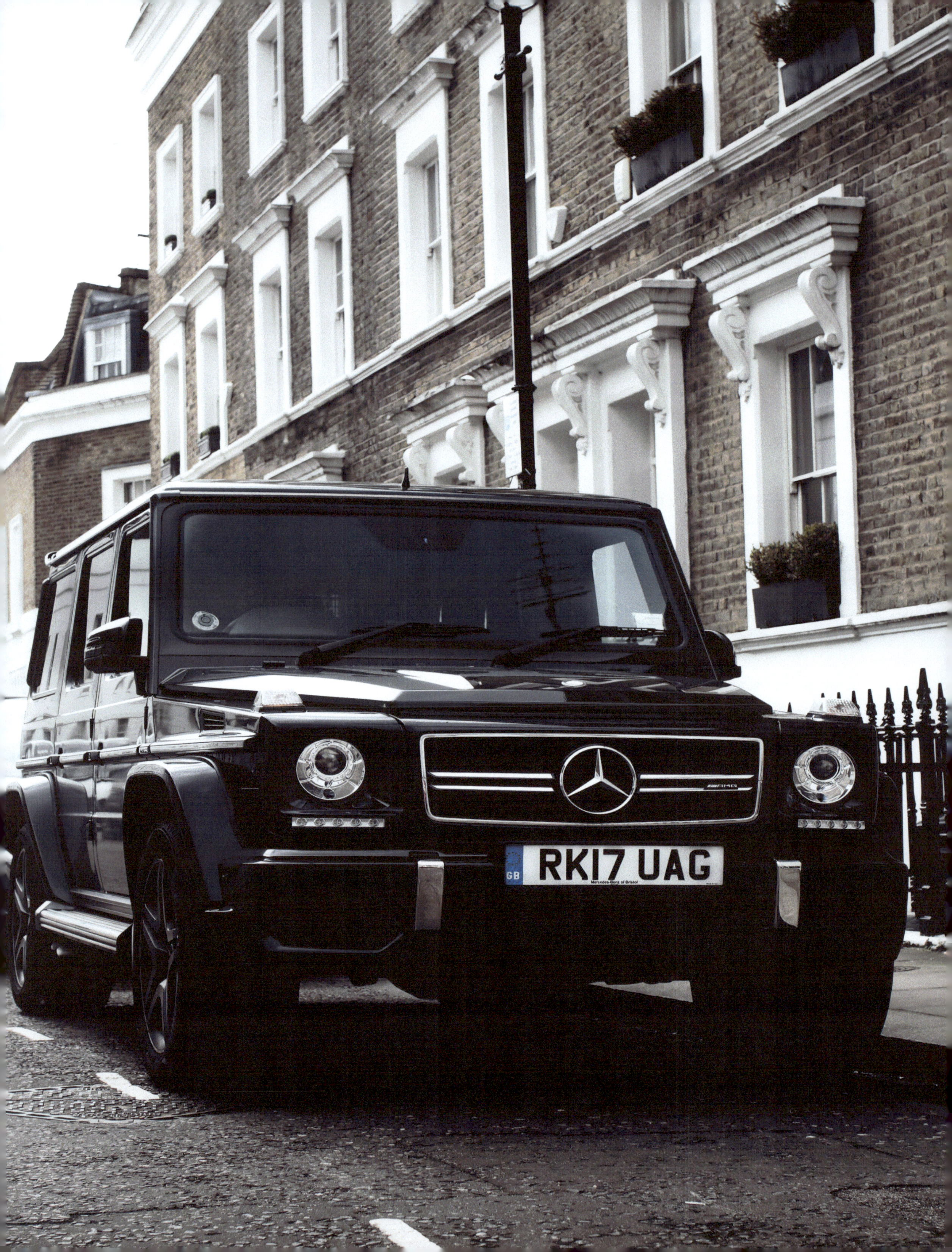
GB
RK17 UAG
Mercedes-Benz of Bristol

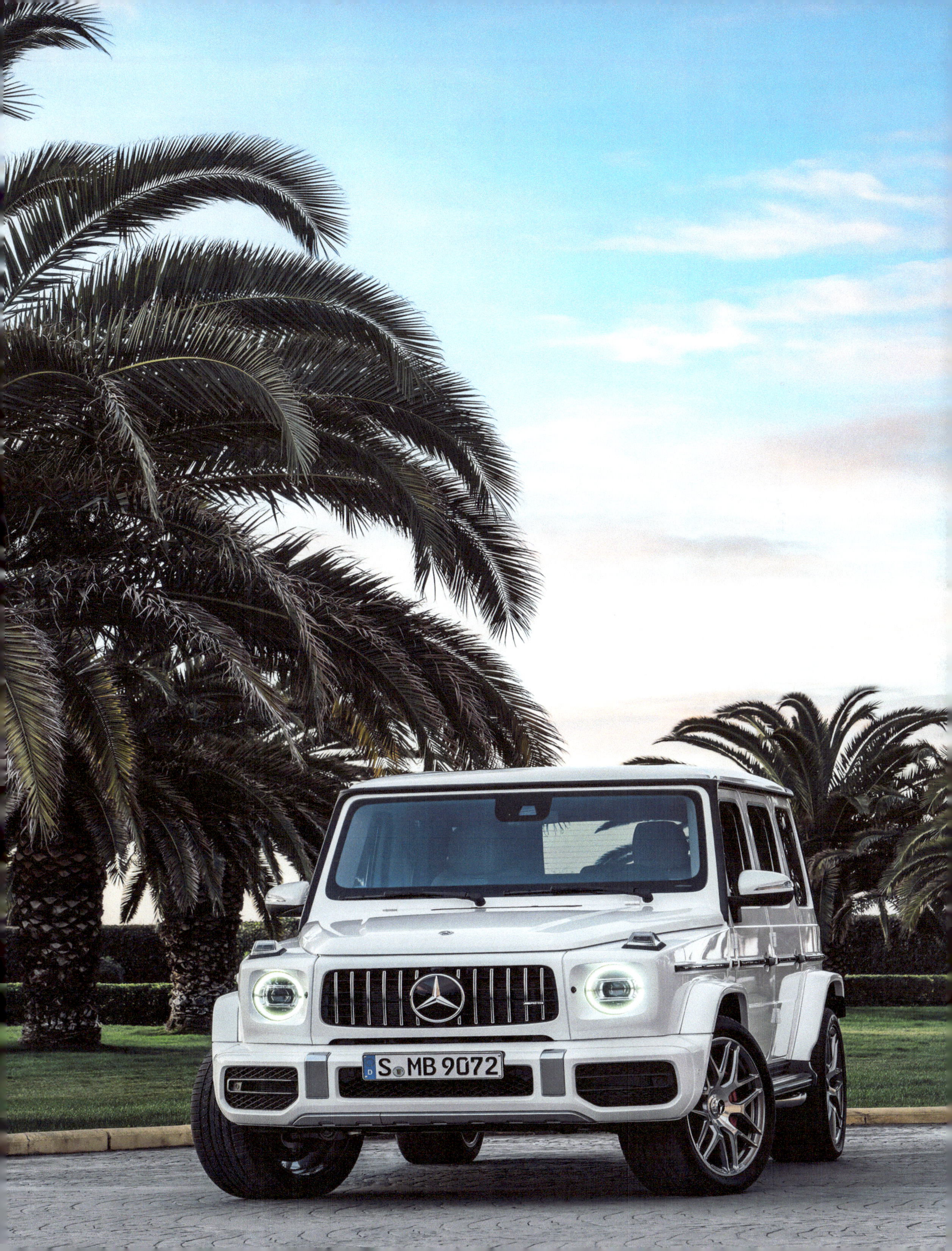
S MB 9072

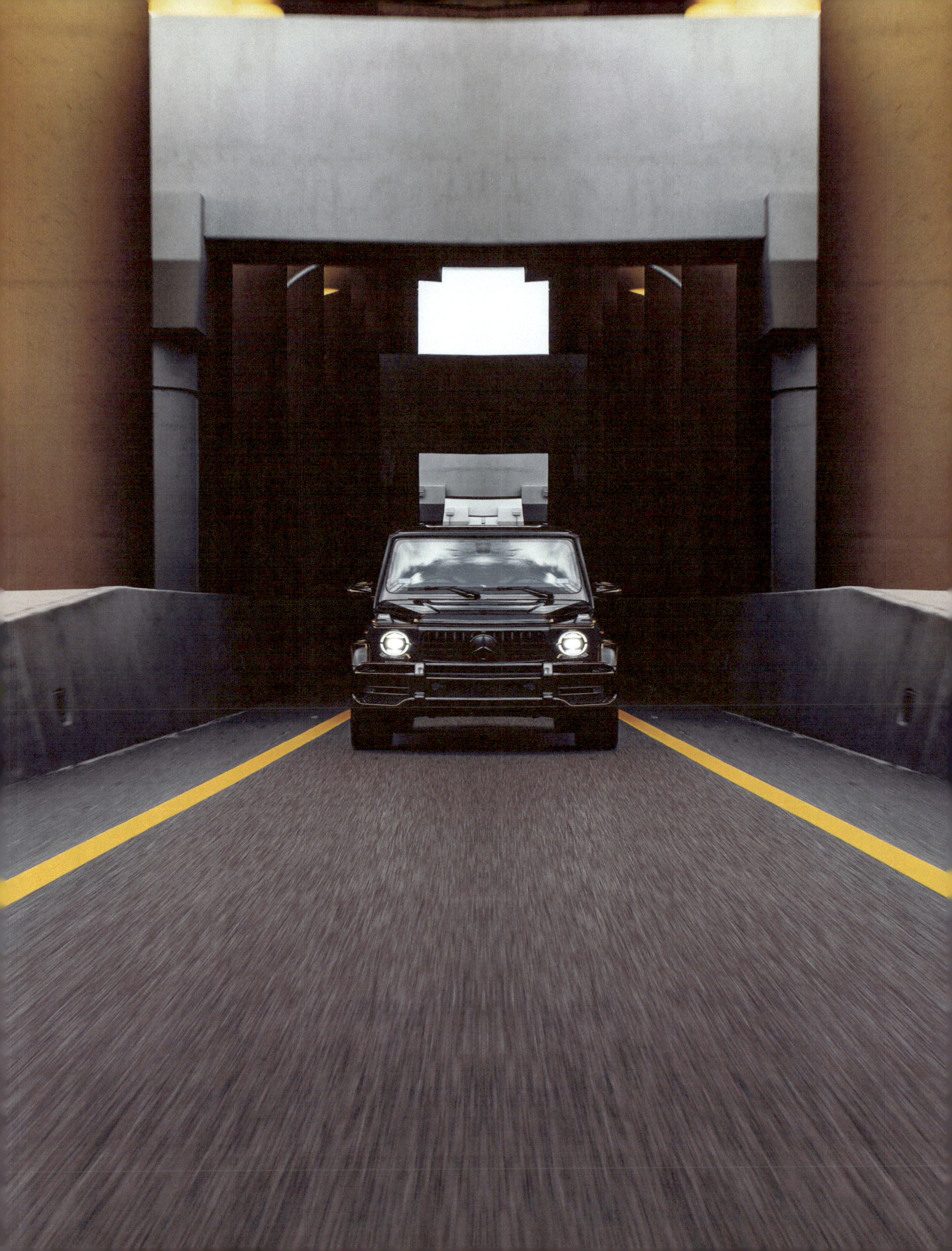

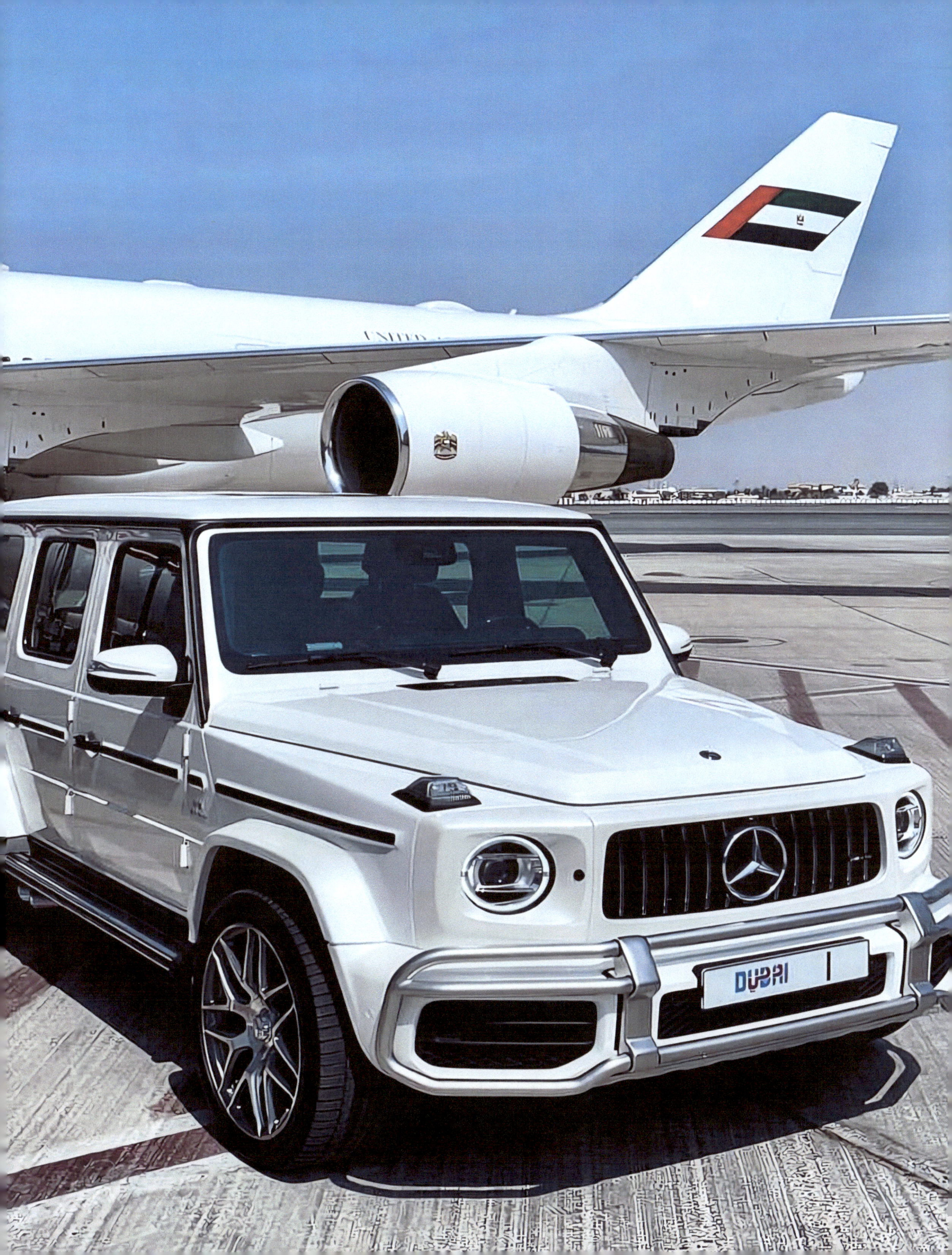
DUBAI

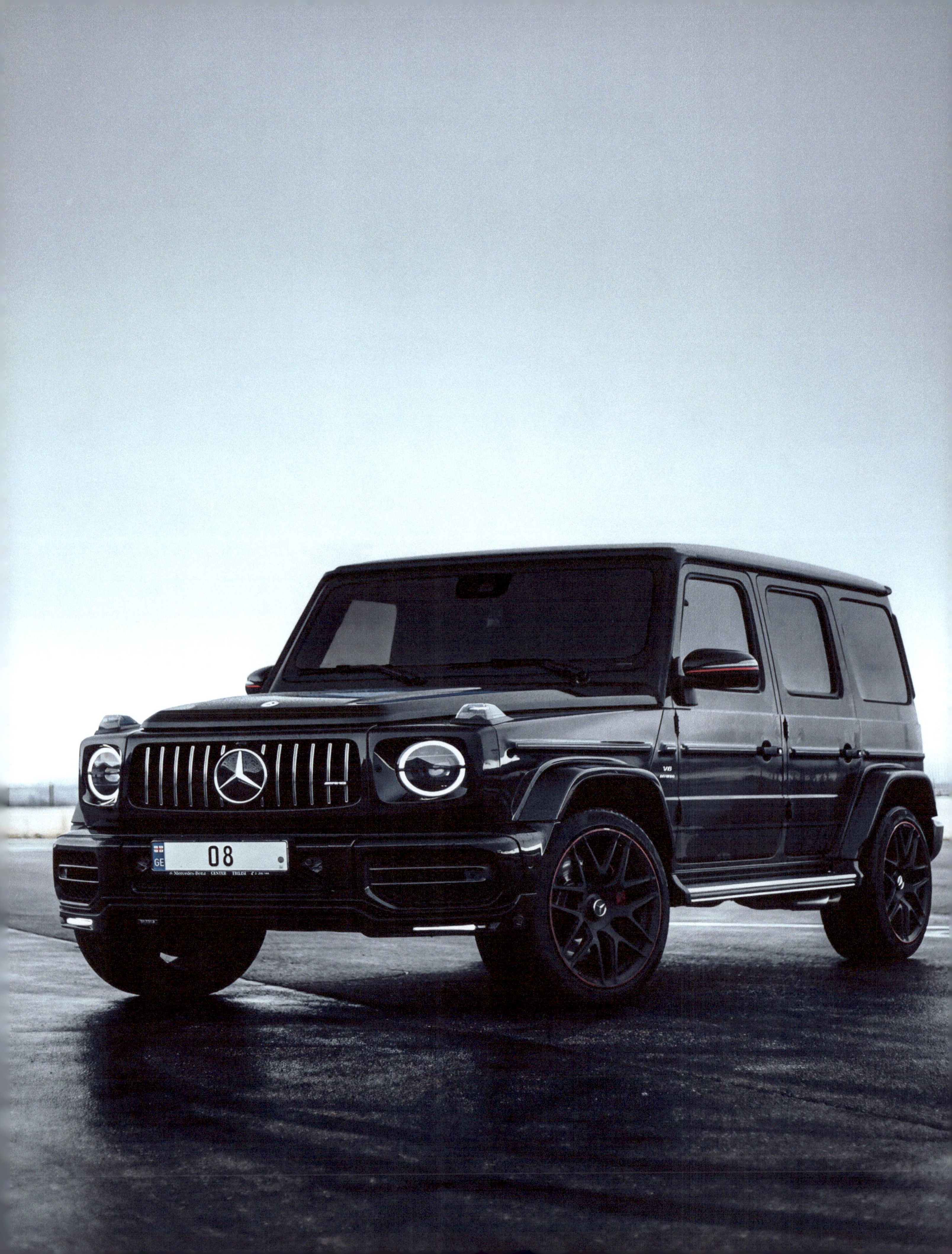
GE
08

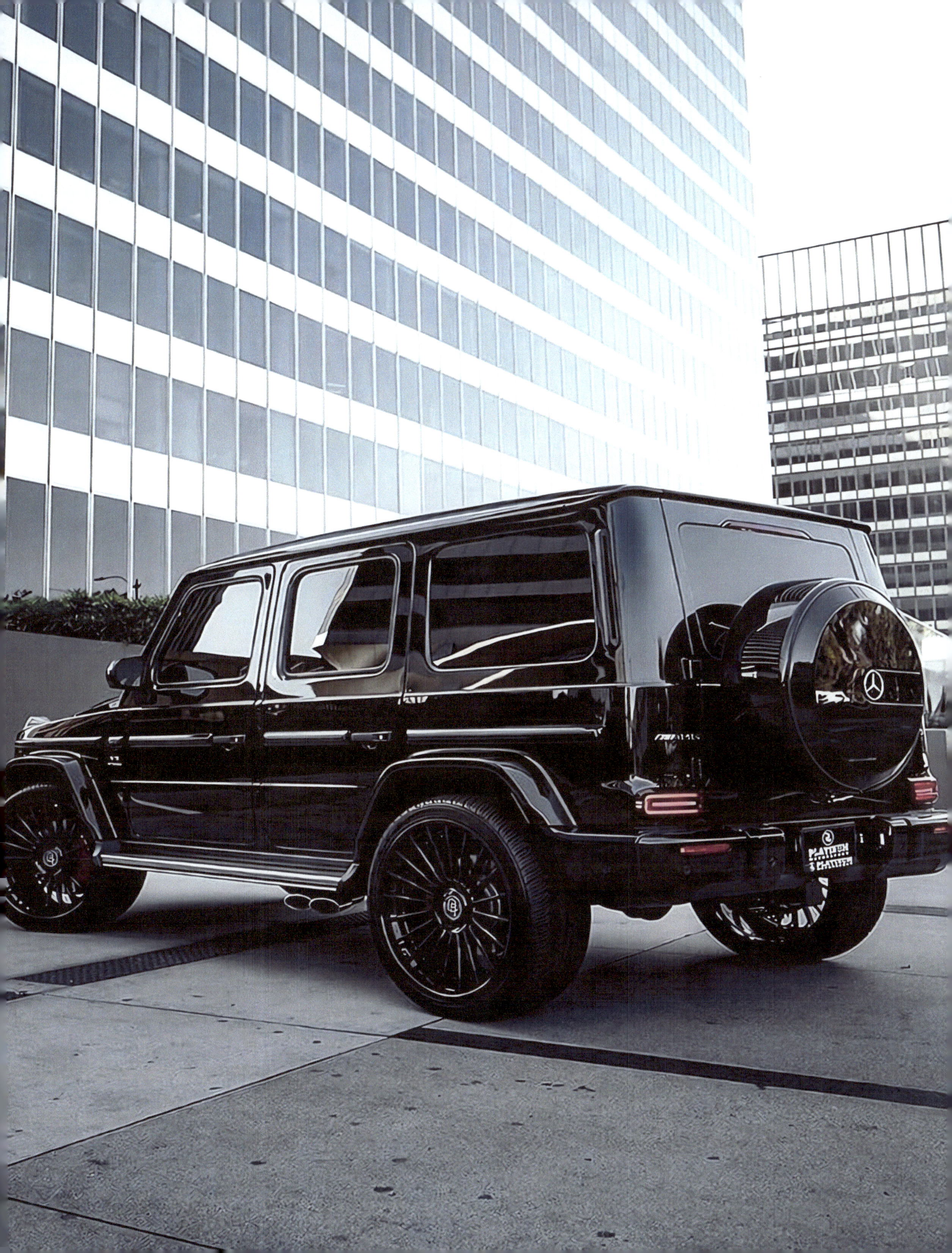

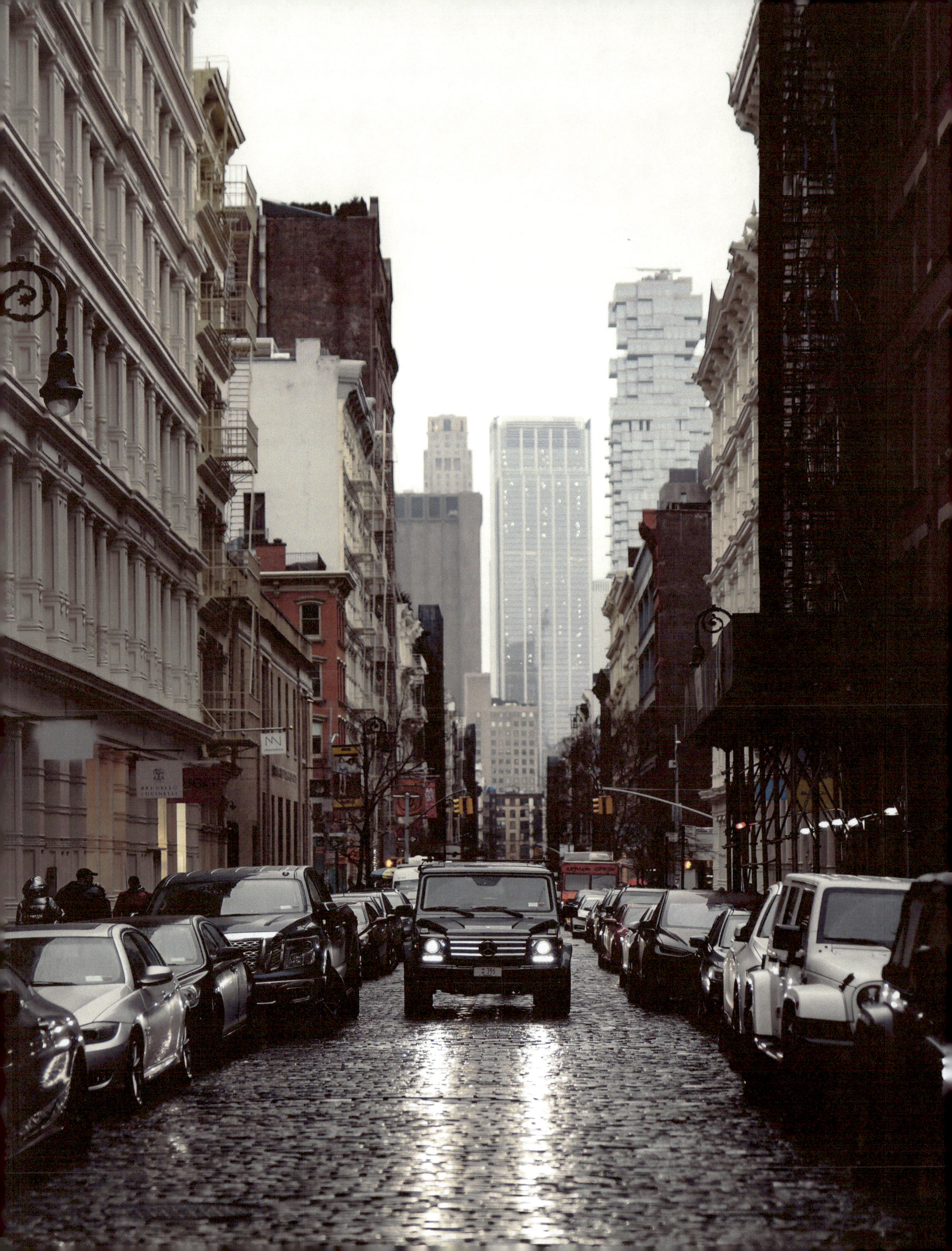
BRUNELLO
CUCINELLI

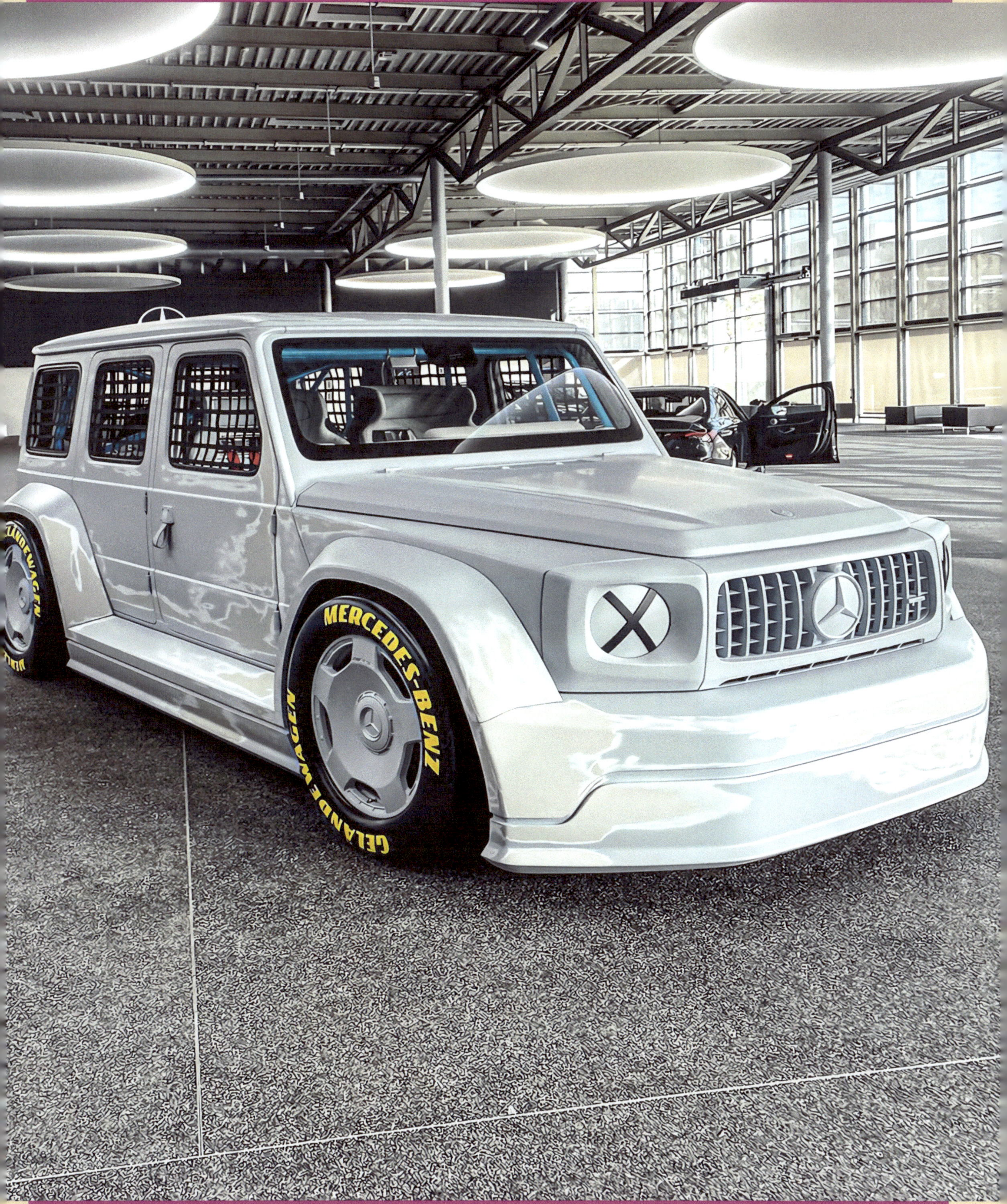
MERCEDES-BENZ
GELANDEWAGEN

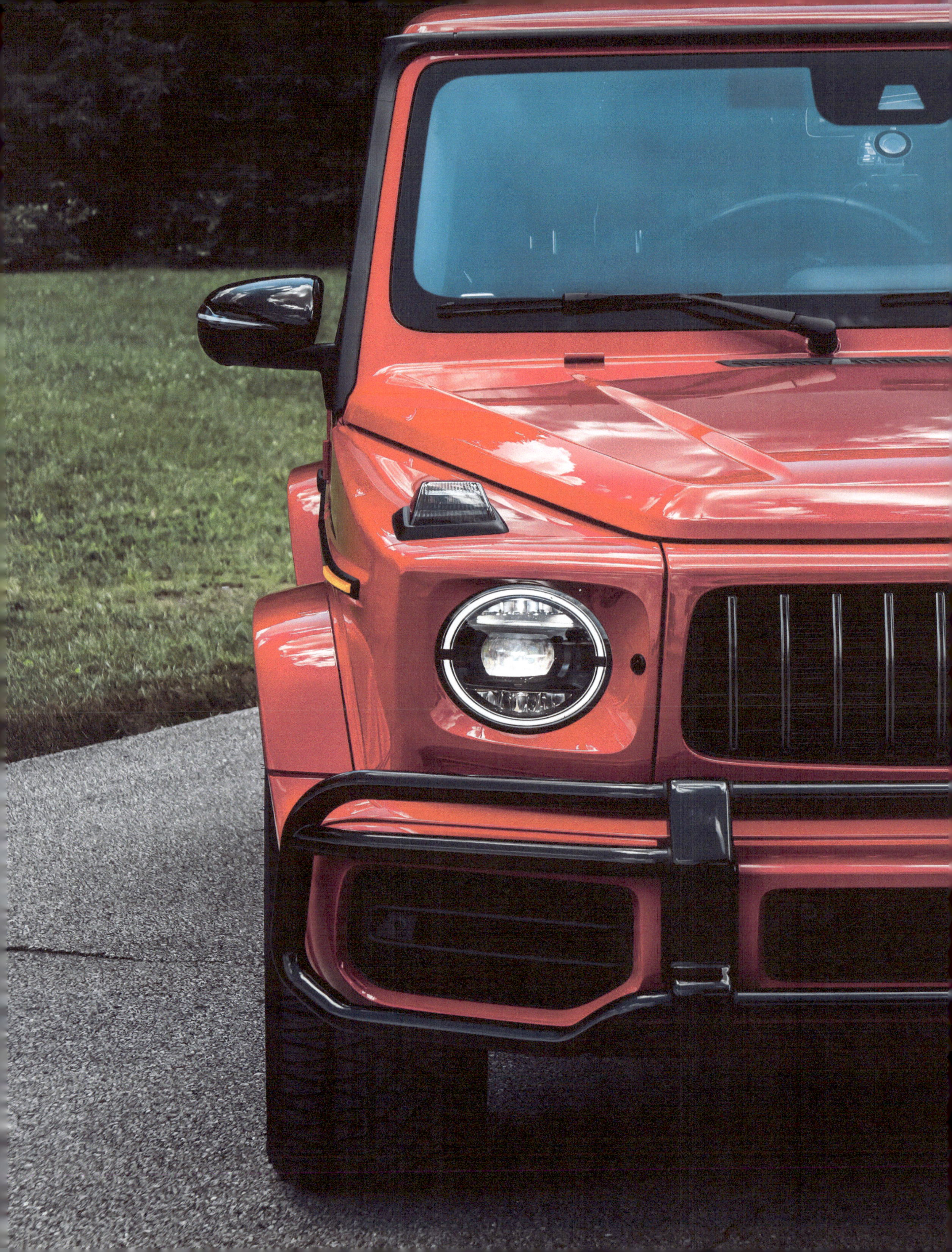

www.ingramcontent.com/pod-product-compliance
Lightning Source LLC
Chambersburg PA
CBHW051827210526
45473CB00005B/1767
9798303103023